Star
in the Hood

By Christopher Lynn Petty

DORRANCE
PUBLISHING CO
EST. 1920
PITTSBURGH, PENNSYLVANIA 15238

Dorrance Publishing Co
585 Alpha Drive
Pittsburgh, PA 15238
Visit our website at www.dorrancebookstore.com

ISBN: 978-88-85272-10-1
eISBN: 978-8-8852-7666-5

Damn, who would've ever thought I'd be living this way? Every place I go brothers are throwing deuces and the "The ladies can't keep their eyes off me". Thugs want to buy out the bar for me while their main girls plot their way to the passenger seat of my new 600 or the gold low-low that I bring out every Sunday. Mothers and fathers who once forbade me from entering their yards are now campaigning for me to wife their daughters or put their sons on. It's funny what money does, but who am I to complain about glamour?

Wasn't easy, though, coming from a small neighborhood in a small town right in the heart of North Carolina! Sanford, one of those towns you breeze by when you're on the highway and you remember seeing the road sign somewhere before. That was then, but now my city rings bells every place you go for various reasons and it's like everyone knows somebody in Sanford. Ask about the Grape Vineyard and you'll notice mixed reactions from the people you ask. Some will remember the 80s and point you in the direction of the peaceful community that they knew it as, while others can only recall the 90s and they'll tell you to be careful where and how you enter this hood because brothers out there are dangerous, especially when strangers enter their gates. The landmark sign that once read "Grapevineyard Road" but now reads "San-Lee Drive." I guess the name change is somehow expected to clog memories or to bring a new identity to our hood. Really, it doesn't matter to me as long as you recognize and respect that this is indeed the "Grapevineyard" and we're still about our business.

Like those with peaceful memories, I too can remember when everything was good in the vineyard. I am a 70s baby; therefore, I was a partaker of all of the fond 80s memories from the hood growing up. All the parents were working in the summertime so the teenagers and the youngsters were on the prowl. Everybody was pretty much sectioned off by age groups and schools but there was always something elite about my group. Notice I said groups, because at this time we weren't noted or perceived as gangs or organizations. We also had the "ol' heads," as we called them, those were the 60s children, you know, the ones who already graduated and were established in the route of life they'd take…. I was somehow depicted the leader of my group; therefore, I made it a law that we'd follow my Uncle Don's generation because they knew how to mix the good with the bad, never allowing the bad to take root in their lives. They never had trouble with the law and I viewed my uncle as the Coolest Cat in the World. He always led his flock. When he'd decide it was a day to chill at the crib and smoke joints all day then his flock would fall into place. When he'd decide that there was a problem that needed to be dealt with they'd still fall into place and get ready to ride on the individuals with whom they had the problem. I admired and took notice to the way that they handled things and I patterned my crew in the same fashion. My Uncle Don is only about 58 inches tall, but he was a player with the women at that time and an enforcer in the streets and with his crew. He and his boys would have the mellow house parties, you know, the ones where Marvin Gaye would be coming out of the speakers and the Chris Tucker would be in the air. Everybody would be calm as they slow danced. When I looked at my uncle I could tell that he was in charge of everything taking place.

My Uncle Don loved me as much as I loved him so he took me under his wing and gave me all of the game. Not only the things that I saw him doing but also he'd answer any questions that I had about how anything else was being done. Like an older brother he'd never tell me what to do or what not to do but when he'd catch me moving too fast he would say, "Nephew, slow down and check yourself!" I had another uncle, Garfield, and he didn't give a damn about anything. Actually he's my great uncle and he had an original "Down South" liquor house. You know, the spot where liquor is poured, drank, and sold all night long...where the aroma of fried chicken is in the air and the sound of cards being shuffled is in every room. Also, the perfect setting for a fistfight to break out and an occasional stabbing if it really got out of hand.

Those were the good ol' days because cats weren't killing each other in the hood at that time. A lot of sex, alcohol, and partying, damn, why didn't the Vineyard remain that way?

My Grandfather June was in control of the card game and he put in a lot of hours at his table. The only time that I could really talk to him was when he'd first wake up and you know how cranky an old man can be when he first gets out of the bed. I was hungry for game so it was natural for me to ask a lot of questions. Grandpa June cussed me out a lot because of all of the questions but it was worth it. I learned a lot from him. Of course, learning the card games topped the list but rules like making the players comfortable and keeping down the conflict was very important. Hundred-dollar table stakes and 10% of the cut were very, very important because as a child, I was serious about the money. All these things were never forgotten, even though not utilized until years later, they were worth their weight in gold.

While the other age groups and their respected leaders were out having fun, I'd have my crew around the hood as I gave them this game that I had soaked up from my people. No doubt, the older boys in the hood would have their days that they would let us chill with them and where they'd give us a little game. My cousin Clarence was the leader of his squad and they had a lot of love for us because they knew that we looked up to them. We never told anyone when we'd see them doing wrong. When you'd see Clarence, you would know that Pat, Stanley, Amos, and Arnold weren't far off.

Sometimes you would see my Aunt Kim because she was thugged out and would roll harder than the guys at times.

My squad was few but since we stuck so close together it made us a strong unit. My man Rome (called Blake) was the loose cannon even as a child so we had to keep an eye on him. My cousin Frank (called Bo Jack) was always relaxed but he was the most dangerous person that I have ever met. My name is Allen but the hood has always known me as Bo. Uncle Don gave me that nickname. It stuck with me throughout my life. We had a few other guys from the Vineyard in our crew but when it came down to it, it was the three of us who handled business. We found this out when we were teenagers and I'm glad it happened early. We were in this other hood one day shooting ball and we beat the guys in front of all of their lil' girlfriends and their pride got in the way. They copped an attitude and wanted to fight. When they did all of the other guys ran back to the Vineyard. Luckily for Blake, Bo Jack, and me, Clarence and his boys heard that we had some problems and they were there before things popped off!!!

We learned a lot that day and we made a pack that we'd always be down for each other. Win or lose, right or wrong, up or down, we'd be in it together. After that run-in with those guys we all bought a "Troop force jacket" and it symbolized our vow to go down together. Anytime we left the Vineyard, whether together or solo, we'd each have on our jackets. Without having to say it, it was evident to people in town because they'd make comments like "There's your boys over there."

We began getting our hustle on around 1986 and although I was the youngest I was still the shot caller. We did everything from cutting neighborhood yards to selling weed at school, but at the end of the day we'd chop all the money up equally. Even at such a young age our rule was never be flashy, stay humble, and stack as much paper as possible. Bo Jack and Blake were both two years older than me. In 1987 they both were able to get driver's licenses. Before they even started making plans to buy whips, I planted the seed in their head that we'd buy one car together and they'd have to compromise whenever one of them had a date with a young lady. When the time came around for their 16th birthdays we put our money together and snatched up a 1982 Cadillac and it was on and popping from that moment. We put down the lawnmowers because we were mobile now and graduated to the school of the real hustlers.

Uncle Don began treating me like a man and he introduced me to a weed connect. I didn't let the rest of the squad know who the connect was but no doubt, we did our business together and kept everything equal amongst us. The only problem I had was when I'd have to re-up on the weed I'd have to go alone. I didn't feel comfortable in the weed spot without my boys because if anything ever popped off I knew they'd have my back. On one particular evening things did go wrong just as I had feared, but luckily I made it out safely with no scars. What happened was I was in the back room of Will's house (the connect) handling our business as usual. I gave him the money for ten pounds of marijuana and we were waiting for his boys to bring it in from the stash spot outside. As we waited three men kicked the door off the hinges waving pump shotguns in our face. They demanded us to give them the money and weed but Will shouted, "We don't have anything!" Before he could get all of the words off his lips one of the stick-up kids hit him over his eye with butt of the shotgun. He was out like a light. They quickly emptied his pockets of all of the money that I'd just given him. Another one of them turned and walked toward me and when he did I simply said, "I just gave him that money and that was all that I had, so there's no need to shake me down!" Although all of this happened suddenly it was like slow motion to me. As I lay on the floor of Will's house I observed a lot of things. First, as I glanced out of the window of the door I could see Will's boys standing there in the shadows making no attempt to help us. Second, although the robbers wore masks, I looked into their eyes and I recognized one of them. Last, but not least, once the guys fled into the night Will's boys reentered the house pretending that the stick-up kids had hit them also and took all of the weed in the stash. So there I was sitting there while Will's eye was bleeding, his boys crossing him, and the stick-up kids got away with my money. As I rose to leave Will assured me he'd make things right between us when he got straight again and I knew he would because he was a real "G" from the ol' school and his word was bond!!

When I got back to the Vineyard I got at Bo Jack and Blake and they were both in my yard in three minutes. I described to them the events that happened in detail and without saying, we all knew we had business to handle. They also knew the guy that I recognized at Will's house and we knew he'd be at a party that they were having at the armory later that night. Blake had the keys to the Cadillac so I told them both to go get fresh and Blake was to pick us both up in two hours! When they went home to get dressed I went to one of the 06s in the hood, Pat was his name. Pat was a cool ol' head but he had a problem with drugs. He took care of his household but all of his extra money was used to snort powder. He was a real gangsta back in the day and word was that he stayed high a lot because he was tormented by his conscience from all of the people that he had killed. We had a spot in the Vineyard called "The Garage," which the O.G.s claimed was filled with bodies with the majority belonging to Pat. Because of the rumors most people didn't want to be around him but in the hood he got much love and respect. I never asked him about any of the stories that I had heard but the vibe he gave off and the feeling that I'd get when around him, it was like I knew in my gut that he was a killer.

Pat was also good at reading people and it showed when I entered his house on this night. Normally he'd tell me to sit down as he tossed his corny jokes at me but not this time. I don't know if I had a particular look on my face but he told me to step down into his basement and he'd be right there. After ten minutes or so of waiting he joined me in the basement carrying a six-pack of Bull in one hand and a black case in the other. As we popped the beers he spoke to me in riddles but I understood well just what he was saying. Two things stuck with me, he said, "There can only be one chief in the tribe and he must be willing to kill or die for that tribe!" He said, "Sometimes you may have to kill a member of the tribe in order to save the tribe." I never forgot those words. He then opened the case that he had and it possessed a nine-millimeter pistol that was filed down and ready for the streets! He said to me, "Lil' home, you're the next king of these streets so don't hesitate to handle whatever it is you have on your mind." We finished off the six-pack and as I walked off of his porch he told me to be safe and to holla if I need him, ever!!

When I returned around the block to the crib, Bo Jack and Blake were in my backyard drinking some beers of their own. Troop jackets in place. I hurried in the house to get in uniform.

We hopped in the whip and headed for the party at the armory but not many words were spoken during the ride there. Once we found a parking place on the back row in the cut we finished off the beer that my boys had. Still nothing was said about the business. We came there to handle when we finished off our drinks, we stepped inside the party and split up because that was our normal routine.

About an hour inside the club I noticed "Stack" standing at the bar buying rounds for everyone standing around. Stack was the guy that I had recognized from the robbery and when you look at him you can tell by his demeanor that he can't be trusted. He's about six feet two inches tall with a slender build but what stands out most is the fact that he never looks you in the eyes when you're talking to him. I made my way over to the bar and when he noticed me immediately told the bartender to give me one of what he was drinking. Being kinda slick with my tongue I told him, "Thanks, Stack, I guess you knew that I couldn't afford to buy one since you jacked me for all of my paper when I was at Will's house!" When I said that I saw his heart fall into his sneakers and he was so frightened that he didn't even think to deny what I had said to him.

Instead he began to stutter and said, "It wasn't my idea and we had orders not to touch you, why do you think no one hit you like we did Will?" I moved a little closer to Stack and he thought that I was about to hurt him, so he lifted both hands and said to me, "I have your money outside in my car, c'mon and I'll give it to you now and I'll tell you how this all transpired!" I agreed to listen so Stack and I exited the side door of the armory so that no one could see us leave.

We sat down in Stack's car and as he counted out the money I lost in the ordeal he said to me, "Listen, bro, I apologize for knocking you off like that but who wouldn't get down on a free lick? Your boy Blake put us down on the business that you and Will handled and told us to stick you and Will for your paper while he and his cousin who works for Will removed all of the weed from Will's stash spot. They let me keep this change and gave me one pound of weed each!!"

I couldn't believe what he'd just told me, well, let's say I hated to hear what he told me. I said, "Stack, you expect me to believe that my homie that I grew up with set me up to be robbed, besides, I never told him who my connect was?"
Stack replied, "I'm telling you, man, his cousin works for Will and they put the whole thing together to get your money and Will's weed!"

My plan had been to take all of Stack's money and jewelry and to whip him with my pistol but the words he'd just spoken to me took all of my strength away. I simply said to him, "I won't put your name in the streets as being a stick-up kid long as you keep everything you just told me on the hush!" He agreed so I stepped out of his car and went back inside the party.

Soon as I entered the building two girls from the hood rushed me and told me that Bo Jack was at the bar having words with somebody. I rushed to the bar area and found Rod, Blake's cousin who worked for Will, standing behind the bar pleading with Bo Jack that he didn't know anything about what Bo Jack was saying. Normally we would've rolled on Rod but after receiving the news that I received I told Bo Jack to let it go and let's go home.

I scanned the area quickly to locate Blake but he wasn't anywhere to be found. Any other time he'd be somewhere close to Bo Jack but I knew if I mentioned it to him he'd say he didn't want to be involved because it was his cousin and his homie who were having words. I sent one of the home girls to find him and tell him that Bo Jack and me would be at the car waiting on him. Once Blake arrived at the car I told them we should all go home for the night because I had a feeling that things weren't right inside the party. I also told them that Stack approached me, gave me my money, and told me if he had known that I was inside the house he never would've been a part of it.

The situation was dead in everybody's eyes, except for mine, because now I knew that one in my family couldn't be trusted. I had to keep it to myself. Bo Jack was still thinking about doing things to Stack but anytime the subject was brought up I'd notice Blake's head drop. From that night on I never saw Blake in the same way and I'd never allow him to know about any moves that I was making. I still broke bread with him and made sure that he was making money but I couldn't help the love that was lost. I wondered if he'd strike again given the opportunity and I often pondered what the homie Pat had said about killing one in the tribe but I'd quickly eliminate that thought because it wasn't in my heart to hurt Blake. It was obvious to me at times that his conscience was getting the best of him so I was hoeing that guilt would prevent him from ever pulling another stunt like that one.

By 1991, we were all living comfortably but not hanging out the way that we used to. Mostly for business, aside from that we didn't do too much as a group. Bo Jack had married his wife Cheri and had two beautiful kids. He spent most of his time at home. I'd stop by their house a couple times a week to play video games with the kids but then I'd keep it moving. Blake had three kids himself, all by different women, but he spent a lot of time at house parties and hole-in-the-wall clubs. He was blowing a lot of money at these spots and he lost discipline on the rule of stacking and staying lowkey. He'd often get into fights late in the night and call me and Bo Jack to come to his aid. We both sat him down and told him we'd outgrown fighting for no reason and he needed to do the same. I was still single at the time and since I had no kids and was able to travel a lot. I spent a lot of time in Richmond, VA, with my partner Jay. I met him through Will a few years earlier. Jay was old enough to be my father but for some reason we hit it off from day one. At first he was selling heroin at a low-low price but then it led to me meeting his family. Will couldn't believe how deep Jay had let me in because he had known him for years and had never even been to his house. Jay was undoubtedly the most dangerous person that I had ever met. He wouldn't hesitate to kill and he would tell you that himself. None of that ever bothered me because I had learned from my uncle early in life that long as you respected people, for the most part, you would get that respect in return.

I made Jay a lot of money so to show his appreciation he invited me on a Florida trip with him and his family. Miami for three weeks, it sounded good to me since I had never stayed out of town for longer than a week. Jay's oldest daughter, Stephanie, picked us from the airport. She and her mother lived in Miami. Jay, his wife, Donna, and two teenage sons, David and Jeremy, were busy laughing and catching up with Stephanie on the drive to the motel.

Meanwhile, Stephanie and I were busy eye flirting. Jay noticed our eye contact. When we arrived at his beach house he told Stephanie to take me to meet her mother and show me around. He got his family settled in while we were gone. Prior to this trip Jay had never mentioned Stephanie to me. It was a relief that Jay was cool with the friction building between Stephanie and me.

Stephanie's mother was half Cuban and Stephanie had the long silky jet-black hair. She was very talkative and although two years older than me she had the youthful look of a teenager. She was very intelligent too. She worked at City Hall in Dade County and owned three condos in Opa Locken that she rented out. I learned all of this over the 20-minute drive to her mother's house. To my surprise, Jay had told her a lot about me over the years, so it was starting to feel like this vacation was really a love connection that Jay had set up himself. Whatever, it turned out to be would be cool with me because I came to Miami for R & R and that's exactly what I planned to do. I told Stephanie a little more about myself during the drive and she appeared to like what she saw and heard. I made it clear to her that I felt really fortunate to be in this position.

Finally we arrived at her mother's house. Maria's house looked like one of the mansions from the television show Miami Vice. When we entered the house, to my surprise, Maria said, "You must be Bo, whom I've heard so much about from Stephanie and Jay. I thought I would've met you by now. You know how cautious my ex-husband is when it comes to bringing people around his family. He thinks highly of you and I know someone else who has thoughts of you" (pointing at Stephanie as they both laughed). Stephanie, blushing, said, "My mother is always trying to embarrass somebody." Finally I told Maria it was nice to meet her as well and I was looking forward to my three weeks in Miami. She insisted that I stay at her home but I told her that I had better stay close to Jay.

After Stephanie and I had cruised the strips of Miami, she talked my ears off for over an hour. She drove me back to her father's place so that I could settle in. Donna and the boys were already out on the beach. Jay and Stephanie used that time to get a little father-daughter time in. I showered and unpacked. I called Bo Jack to let him know that my flight went well and that I thought that I was really gonna enjoy myself down in the bottom. Bo Jack informed me that he didn't have much work left and he may need me to cut my vacation short. I told him that was out of the question. I told him to get that thought out of his mind. I also told him about Stephanie. I told him that she could possibly be the "one." Bo Jack laughed and said, "Yeah, right!" I ended the conversation short in order to get some rest because Stephanie had already told me that she was on three weeks' vacation from work so I knew that I would need my energy.

The next morning I woke up early when I heard Jay's voice in a panic like I had never heard before. He was standing at the window in my room (where his family couldn't hear him) having a telephone conversation. I pretended to be asleep but I heard him saying things like "How long do I have and when can I come and see you?" I couldn't put my finger on what was really going on but I began to mentally prepare myself for something other than relaxation in my immediate future. When he left my room I got myself together and found him standing on the balcony of the beach house. I asked Jay what was wrong. I did not let him know that I had overheard his telephone conversation. He told me to get ready because his baby had plans for the two of us. Jay pretended that nothing was wrong.

Stephanie called and said that she would be by to pick me up in an hour so that we could go out on a boat. I used my time to have breakfast with Donna and the boys at a nearby café. Jay said that he didn't feel much like eating. As we sat down to eat I noticed that Donna was twisting her fork 'round and 'round and that her mind seemed to be someplace in outer space. When the boys finished their plates I gave them some money to go next door to the tackle shop to but some fishing equipment so that we could do some fishing later in the week.

When they left us alone I asked Donna to tell me what was going on. She lifted her head and stared at me for a few seconds and then she burst into tears. I moved around the table to put my arms around her because she was so weak that she would've fallen out of the chair. Finally she gathered herself and asked if I knew why we had come to Miami. I told her that we had come for a vacation. Stephanie told me that she wished that were the truth. She went on to tell me how Jay had been using his own product for the past year or so and had created so much debt that they were about to lose all of their properties in both Richmond and Miami, including the house that Stephanie and Maria lived in.

We sat in silence for a moment then I asked her how much debt was he in. She told me that Jay owed his supplier in Miami one and a half million dollars and that he refused to give Jay any more work until his debt was paid in full. He had been given until the end of the month to pay his debt or his people would take away everything that Jay owned. I asked her if anyone else knew and she told me that Jay was supposed to tell the others at dinner tonight! I knew it wouldn't be long before Stephanie came by to pick me up, so I gathered Jay's boys from the tackle shop and we hurried back to the beach house. Donna asked me not to mention any of this to Jay until he broke the news to everyone at dinner that night.

When we got back to the beach house Stephanie was already there waiting for me. She was sitting on the hood of her Baby Benz with an orange bikini on. She was talking with her dad, who was standing a short distance away from her. The bikini that Stephanie wore, along with long black hair and baby doll eyes, was not enough to get my mind off of the news that was just dropped on me. Jay, still holding his composure, told me us to have fun but to make sure that we were back in time for the eight-o'clock dinner that he had planned. I hopped into the passenger seat of Stephanie's whip and as we drove off I looked through the mirror at Jay and all that I could think of was that I had to do something to help him and his family out. I know that he would do the same for me. I knew that it would not be easy because for one, I had never dealt with that kind of money before and two, now that Jay was cut off from his supplier, I too would be out of work.

Stephanie and I went to the dock, where we chattered about for hours. I couldn't take my eyes off of this beautiful woman and the things that she said were so deep that she had my undivided attention.

Even though we had our laughs and learned even more about each other, Stephanie could still tell that my mind was occupied by something else. "Why have you drifted into silence on me?" she asked. I apologized and told her that I had some things on my mind that I needed to deal with. She told me that if I wanted to talk about it to let her know but I reassured her that it was nothing serious.

Dinnertime was approaching so Stephanie and I headed back to the house to get changed for dinner. Stephanie took a different route to her dad's house and we by passed mostly gated communities and I could see the Mandivas from the interstate. She pointed out different houses of her friends and associates. She pointed out Darren's house. She told me that it was the one with the lights around it. I asked her who Darren was. She said, "You mean that you haven't met Darren yet after all of the money you and my dad have made him?" I smiled because I didn't know her dad shared so much information with her. I said that I had never met him but could she introduce them to each other. She said sure and we took the next exit, which took us to his house.

I don't know what possessed me to ask her to take me there but it was too late to change my mind. We were already at his gate and Stephanie was pushing buttons as if she stopped by her frequently. I guess that she knew what I was thinking because she was like "Darren is my Godfather and his code hasn't changed since I was a teenager." I thought to myself, Godfather, how could a Godfather put his goddaughter and her mother out on the streets, but I held that to myself.

As we drove around his circular driveway a tall, slender black man with dreadlocks halfway down his back was walking toward the car with a smile on his face. "Who is he?" I said, and Stephanie told me that it was Darren. I was shocked because for some reason any time Jay mentioned his Miami connect, I automatically assumed that it would be someone of a Hispanic descent. Normally when a person is handling as much work as Darren it is a person from across the Atlantic.

Before Stephanie could stand up straight Darren had already embraced her and kissed her on her cheek. "Who's your friend?" Darren asked. She said, "Bo," and before she could say any more Darren said, "Oh, you're the youngun who made Jay rich, huh?" We shook hands firmly as he stared into my eyes and I said, "If you call it rich."

He asked us inside but Stephanie told him that we couldn't because we had to be at her dad's for dinner by eight o'clock. Darren and I shook hands again and he told me he'd like to sit down and talk to me before I left Miami. I asked Darren if tomorrow sounded good to him and he instructed his goddaughter to bring me by at ten. She said that she would and we got into the car so that we wouldn't be late for our date with Jay.

When we pulled into Jay's driveway, Stephanie was about to get out of the car but I grabbed her hand and asked her to wait for a minute. I asked her what kind of person that Darren was. She told me that he was a fair man, good with his friends and family, but also he was about his business, even when it was his family and friends. She wanted to know what I was planning. I told her to wait until after dinner and I would explain everything to her.

Stephanie left to go home to change and to pick her mother up for dinner. I showered and got fresh as I tried to prepare my mind for the events that were about to take place. As I stared out of the window in my bedroom, I saw Jay standing at a distance under a tree. He was along with a look on his face as if he had the weight of the world on his shoulders. I couldn't take it any longer watching my friend being pushed deeper into a corner and trying to deal with all of these problems by his self.

By planning this dinner to break the news to his family, it was obvious to me that Jay had given up because he had run out of options. What he didn't factor into his solution was the fact that he had a friend in me, a friend who wasn't about to leave him helpless and alone to deal with all of this. I took a deep breath, and I walked outside to join Jay under the tree.

Unexpectedly I asked Jay if he trusted me and with a forced half-smile he told me that he did and he wanted to know why I had asked. I explained to him that I knew about his problems with drugs and his debt to Darren. I told him that I know that together we could work to correct them both. I said to him, "It's not important who told me because you know that it was told to me out of love, so again, do you trust me enough to work with me?" Humbly and teary-eyed, Jay responded that for the past two years I had proven to be his friend. He told me that if I had a plan to share it with him.

As we spoke, Stephanie and Maria arrived. I told Stephanie that I needed to borrow her car so that her dad and I could go grab a few things from the store. We hopped into the car and drove down to the beach about a mile away and parked under a pier.

I told Jay to just listen as I talked and I explained the situation to him, as I knew it. "I have a meeting with Darren tomorrow," I explained. I went on to explain to Jay that I needed him to accompany me. I told Jay that I knew that Darren wasn't going to give him any more work, so we had to convince him to give me enough work to pay his debt off and to have some change to put in our pockets.

I explained to Jay that we would ask Darren to consider extending the one-month deadline into three months and that Jay would remain in Miami until their faces were straight with him. I had all of my people in North Carolina and his people in Richmond knew me. I explained that I would flood the streets and flip money real fast so that we could get back to our normal way of living. I told Jay to promise me that after all of this was over with, I needed him to enter a rehab until he could conquer his addiction. I also wanted him to pull away from the drug scene. Jay answered me with a "If you pull all of this off, you have my word on both of your requests!" I told him alright and we left for dinner with Jay's family. I told him to toss his planned speech. I assured him that no one was losing any property as far as I was concerned. Jay laughed and said, "Thanks." I jokingly told him I would do anything for my future father-in-law.

When we entered the house with smiles on our faces Donna couldn't believe it. As we prepared to sit down for dinner I pulled Donna aside and told her not to worry because I thought that we had a plan to work everything out.

At the dinner table Donna had prepared for me the seat next to Stephanie so I guess that our interests were obvious to everyone.

After dinner I walked Stephanie and Maria to their car and I told her that her dad was driving me to Darren's the next morning. She asked if everything was well and after assuring her everything was fine, I told her that I would call her after the meeting with Darren. I also told her that I wanted to spend more time with her over the next few days because I would probably end my vacation sooner than expected and return to North Carolina. I saw the disappointment in her eyes, but I quickly let her know that our friendship was only in its beginning stages.

Jay and I were up late that night sitting on the balcony, having a few drinks. I sat at the table with a calculator, pen, and paper because I wanted to have my numbers precise when we sat down with Darren. I knew it'd be much faster and easier to get off cocaine instead of heroin and with the low-low price that Darren had once quoted to Jay, it wouldn't take long to clear Jay's debt and get into a rehab!

I did all of my figuring on paper and showed them to Jay to get his opinion. I saw satisfaction in his eyes as he read the numbers. He said that he did not know why he hadn't thought of this plan himself. Jay went on to say that the way that I had it figured out we would have the money to repay Darren in a month's time plus have $800,00.00 extra.

I said, "What do you mean by we?"

Jay replied, "If Darren agrees to this, which I am sure that he will, I will leave Donna and the kids here and I will return to NC and VA with you to make this faster since I know most of the people! Besides, when they see my face they will know it is no room for games and the money will flow like water. Once the business is handled I will make good of my promises to you and get my life back on track."

I said, "Okay, Jay, let's do it, but right now we need to get some sleep because we have a busy day tomorrow."

When Jay went to his room I called Stephanie and told her to call her Godfather the first thing in the morning to let him know that her dad would be bringing me to his house and I thought he'd be satisfied with our plan. Stephanie continued to ask if everything was alright and I told her that things were good and that she should stop worrying.

The next morning we rose early enough to get some breakfast and to head out to Darren's place. When we arrived at his house he had two guys at the gate waiting on us and they escorted us to the circular driveway that I remember so well. Darren motioned for us to come inside and he led us into his "fun room," which was filled with pool tables, a bar, and a television that was larger than any other that I had seen before.

Darren told us to have a seat, then he said to Jay, "I'm assuming you've told Bo about our situation since you didn't mind joining him for our meeting." Jay told him yes and complimented me by telling him that even though I was young I was the most trustworthy person that he had ever met. Darren replied, "I believe you because I saw that in him the minute that I met him the other day. This is why I asked that he come over. I hope that you explained to him that I am not a bad person but what went on between us was business and I did all that I could for you." That was when I spoke up.

Looking at the both of them I said, "I understand well what

went on between the two of you, which is why I have this plan, which carries me well out of my way just to fix things between the two of you. Without being told, I know you two are close friends, if not, you wouldn't be Stephanie's Godfather and you definitely wouldn't be accepting properties as payment. Also, by me knowing Jay, he wouldn't consider surrendering all that he has to just anybody because we both know that if he didn't have love for you, you'd either have to kill him or take a loss right now. Out of love for Jay and respect for Stephanie, Donna, and Maria, I hope we can put this plan that I have in my pocket in effect so that there won't be any type of loss in this unfortunate situation, especially any loss of love."

I removed the plan from my pocket and handed it to Darren and I explained that the most important part to the plan wasn't written on the paper but it was a promise from Jay stating he would enter a rehab once this business was complete and remain there until he conquered his addiction. I explained to Darren that I only needed sixty days to take care of everything on that paper. Darren glanced at my formula with a smile on his face and passed the paper back to me and told me to explain it to him verbally. I shredded the paper and I said, "What it boils down to is this, if you front me 60 keys at ten grand each, then I'll give you $28,000.00 back off of each keys. Jay and I did the math last night, at this price I would be able to pay you for the shipment and also pay every dime of what Jay owes you."

"What would you get out of this deal?" Darren asked.

"Monetarily, close to 800 grand but it's the bigger picture and the principle that moves me to do this. For one, Jay and his family will keep their assets and we can all focus on Jay getting himself together because I know you want that as much as everyone else. And two, I consider my way of introducing myself to you, because not only will all of your money be straight but it will also show you just how far I will go for my people. Hopefully we both have longevity in mind, since Jay has shut down I will need a connect and I am sure you'd love to have someone you can trust to move the work that Jay has been moving over the years."

Laughing Darren said, "You have it all planned out, don't you?"

Humbly I said, "I think this will work well and work out for everybody but if you have any other ideas I am open to those as well."

Darren poured us all drinks then he came over to sit down next to us. Then he called over to one of the guys who met us at his gate and introduced him to us as "Sin." Darren said that he liked my plan for the most part but Jay would have to remain in Miami until everything was complete, including his drug treatment. "I'll oversee all of his needs as Sin will oversee mine." Darren explained that he could only get his hands on thirty keys at the present time but by the time that I was finished with the thirty that I had he would have thirty more. Sin would contact me daily and when the second set of keys arrived I was to give Sin the cash. Darren asked me when would I be leaving and I said if possible, the next day. Darren proposed a toast to a new beginning for everyone! Darren instructed me to be at his crib the next day at 4:30 P.M. He said that he would put Sin and Me on a plane tomorrow evening but he needed me to give him directions to my house. To my surprise Daren had people in Cumberland County, which was next to me. The picture was beginning to get clearer to me. The shipment would arrive in Cumberland County and then brought to me. Sin was a safety valve so if anything went wrong he would either be witness to the fact or have knowledge of my family's whereabouts! None of which was a problem for me because I was always straight up about my business.

After all of the "cheers" were up I shook hands with Darren as Jay and I prepared to leave. I looked at Sin and told him that he would love N.C. but he would have to leave some of his jewelry at home. Once I heard him laugh I knew that we would get along just fine.

The ball was rolling now and after further thought I decided that I didn't need as many people as I had planned. Jay had a brother in Virginia who bounced in and out of the game. He knew just as many people as Jay. I told Jay to call him, explain the situation, and tell him that I would bring him ten keys to Virginia and pay him ten grand to get them off. Donnell, Jay's brother, was tight but I knew he'd agree to this when he heard it was for his brother. Jay made the phone call and told Donnell to let all of his people know that he would have them for 25 grands real soon. Everything was straight on that end. I called Bo Jack and told him that I would be home sometime the following night and that I needed him to pick Sin and me up from the airport. Of course, he asked who was Sin. I told him that I'd explain all of that when I got home.

Jay and I left Darren's content with our meeting. I told him that I wanted to spend some time with Stephanie before I left Miami and he said that it was cool with him. I said to him, "Jay, I'd never disrespect you in any so I need to know, right now, if you have any discomfort with me spending time with your daughter." Jay responded, "It's all good, soldier. I can tell by the way that she looks at you that she is feeling you. So if my baby doll has to fall for someone, why not you?" We both laughed and I said, "Since it is all good in everybody's eyes, then I'd appreciate it if you would take me by her house! I called her to let her know that I was on the way and I told her to get all of her plans together in a hurry because I would be leaving the next morning." I told Jay to hit me on Stephanie's cell phone in a few hours to let me know all of the flight arrangements. I reminded him that Sin had to be in place when it was time to go.

When we arrived at Stephanie's, she was sitting out front waiting for us. She told us that she'd follow us to Jay's beach house so that I could get my bags packed. She laughed and said that she would be keeping me until it was time for me to go. Maria came outside to hug me and to say goodbye. I told her that "All so-longs are not goodbyes!" Maria understood well what I meant by that statement. We then left for Jay's and during the ride there I told him not to worry about anything because he knew that this wasn't new to me. I told him to sit back, chill, and enjoy Miami while I got that money straight. He told me, "I know you're on top of this, it's just that I feel so terrible for creating this situation for all of us." Jay asked, "How can I ever repay you?" I told him, "You paid me years ago when you became my friend and I'm not doing anything for you that you wouldn't do for me, right?" Jay replied that I knew that was right. We laughed together. We laughed and joked while I packed and told the family that I would see them in a few weeks. Stephanie told her dad that we'd be staying at her vacant condo in Opa Locka. She told Jay to pick me up there. Jay told us to hold on a second while he called the airlines and made flight reservations. This way I would know before we left. He did just that and told me he'd pick me up at 9:30 A.M. because he could get us an 11:00 A.M. flight. He then shook my hand and hugged his daughter, with tears in his eyes as we walked out of his house.

Stephanie and I left in her car to begin a night that I wouldn't soon forget. When we arrived at her condo she had a box in her trunk that was heavier than the luggage that I had packed.

The inside of her crib was so lavish that it made me think to myself that I really needed to step my game up. I mean, the Italian leather furniture, marble floors, walk-in closets and the step-up jacuzzi in her bedroom had me making plans for my own as soon as I saw Stephanie's.

After giving me a tour of her place, Stephanie began unpacking her heavy box that she had taken out of her car. I did not know until tonight that there were so many types of candles. She started placing them in every corner of her bedroom. She then removed a bottle of Monet. Now I knew why the box was so heavy. I put the bottle of "Mo" on ice and Stephanie told me to c'mon, that we needed to run down to the "mini-mall" to pick up some food for her to prepare. I said, "Oh, you can cook too!" She replied, "There's a lot you'll learn about me if you stick around long enough!" Little did she know that I was anxious to learn more about her because everything that I'd seen this far, I loved.

While Stephanie was in the grocery store I went inside Circuit City to grab a movie to watch on her big-screen television that I had discovered in her den. I figured the movie Love and Basketball was fitting for a slow-paced evening with a beautiful woman and a bottle of Monet. I also decided to take her to the old school by snatching up one of my favorite "oldie CDs" by "Guy." It contained the hit "Let's Chill" but it was one of those tapes you could press play and let it ride. I threw my things in the car and went inside the store to help Stephanie with her bags and also to get me a six-pack of Heineken. Why not, I figured if I was going to drink, I might as well fall all of the way back. When we got back to the condo I threw in the "Guy" CD and sipped on my Heineken as I watched Stephanie steam crab legs and prepare her own fresh tossed salad. I was in awe of her class but I didn't let it show. We had dinner under the candlelight and the Monet immediately sent me into my comfort zone. In that state of mind I was more alert and I listened to her questions in more detail. It was then that I realized that this lady was trying to really get into my world, from my past to my present, so I knew that she was investigating for more than just a fling. I gave her the answers she needed and I did a bit of inquiring of my own. We moved from the dinner table to the sofa as we snuggled and watched Love and Basketball. Slipping deeper into my zone from the "MO" I chose what seemed to be the perfect scenes in the movie to whisper "sweet nothings" in her ears. It appeared that my mouthpiece was a point that might because after each breath into her ear, the beautiful Stephanie snuggled closer and tighter under the arm. I had around her. When the movie ended Stephanie was going in a shower so I grabbed another Heineken and stepped out on her patio to get some fresh night air. I guess thoughts of the upcoming work that I had to do caused me to drift off because before I knew it Stephanie had walked up behind me and put her arms around my waist. I didn't even hear her coming onto the patio. When I turned and looked at her I was like "Damn," this woman was flawless. Normally a person who is so perfect outwardly is flawed inwardly. In fact, Stephanie seemed to be more beautiful on the inside and I was so mesmerized by everything about her. She had the submissive look in her eyes as if she was saying, "Take me and do whatever you want to do to me!" She grabbed my hand and led me into her bedroom where she sat down on her bed. I said, "Hold on, I want you to hear something." Still tipsy, I staggered into the living room to get my "Guy" CD and popped it in the player. I went to my song "Let's Chill" and told her to listen to the words carefully. I leaned back on the bed with her. I put my head onto her lap so that I could see her eyes. Well, briefly, because I had to close my eyes in order to stop the room from spinning. While "Guy" was doing what they do I was lying there wondering if Stephanie was wearing anything under that T-shirt! As the song ended I was about to ask Stephanie what did she think of the song and water dropped onto my lip. I opened my eyes and Stephanie had a tear running down her cheek. I asked her what was that about and she told me that she's just a water head and those tears that I felt and saw only meant that she was enjoying her evening. Still sporting that "take me" look I sat up, put my arm around her, and I did something that I had never done before with any woman. I looked into her eyes and I told her that she'd given me a feeling that I had never felt before. I knew that there was something special about her. I let her know that as bad as I wanted to make love to her, right there and then, I thought it would be best to wait for me to come back to Miami. Without denying how bad that she wanted me as well, she said, "I can understand that and I respect you even more for that. I don't want anything to go wrong with what I see happening." I told her that I shared her vision, and we fell asleep in each other's arms listening to "Guy"!

The next morning I woke up early but Stephanie wasn't lying next to me anymore. I smelled food so I walked in the kitchen. I found Stephanie cooking breakfast. She greeted me with a kiss and said, "I was gonna surprise you in bed but you've spoiled the surprise!"

I jumped into the shower so that I could get it together a little. Then I sat down for breakfast. After breakfast it was time for me to leave. Stephanie asked me if it would offend me if we held hands so that she could pray for my safety. The request touched my heart. She prayed the sweetest prayer and I will never forget it. Her prayer played over and over again in my mind while Sin and I were on our flight to N.C.!!

Back at home it was all good. Blake and Bo Jack picked Sin and me up from the airport shortly after noon. We stopped by my mom's crib so that she could see my face and know that I was safe because she'd cop a nasty attitude if she heard that I was home before she saw me herself. After introducing Sin to everyone, we had to sneak away from the crib because my lil' brother Chuck always wanted to follow me everyplace that I went. He was ahead of his time with intelligence so even though he knew all of the things that I was into, I still wouldn't allow him to be a part of it. Blake and Sin acted as if they'd known each other their entire lives. I was pleased with that because it meant that I wouldn't have Sin stuck up under me at all times. I had business on my mind, and that business was to clear Jay's debt, get Darren's money, and get back down to Miami so that I could continue to build a relationship with Stephanie. I chose my time to speak with Bo Jack while Blake wasn't around because I still wasn't able to open up much of my business with him. Like always, he was gonna eat, but he didn't need to know the hows, whats or whens to anything that was taking place. Finally Blake and Sin went to the Honda dealership to look at some bikes so I used that time to break it all down to Bo Jack. As I was talking to him my cell phone rang. It was Darren on the other end. He asked me if I knew where a Burger King was located on a Horner Boulevard in my town. I told him yes. He told me that his people were down there waiting for me and that they were driving a dually, pulling a racecar with an enclosed trailer. It shocked me because only two days had passed since I had left and I wasn't expecting the shipment for at least a week or so.

I left Bo Jack at the crib and went to Burger King so that Darren's people could follow me home. They were there just as Darren had said. I went and parked beside of them. Before I could get out of the car the driver rolled down his window and said, "Go ahead, I'm right behind you!"

When we got to my house they simply backed the trailer beside of my house, unhooked the trailer and racecar, and said to me, "Darren thought he'd have to send two shipments but everything came through, so here is everything the two of you agreed to." They climbed back inside of the dually and said, "When you are done we will be back to get the car and the money."

To me this was big because I had never been a part of a transaction this heavy. The driver had told me the back wall of the toolbox would slide out and the keys were sectioned off across it.

I went into the house to get Bo Jack because I wanted him to see it. When I slid the back wall of the toolbox off, Bo Jack's eyes lit up because he had never seen so much cocaine at one time. I told him that it was no different than usual; it was just that we had it all at once, instead of making trip after trip to get from Jay.

After putting it to him that way, it also made me rest easier because in all actuality, everything else was the same. I called Jay's brother in Richmond and to my surprise, he had already had 11 kilos sold so I told him that I'd bring 15 his way. This way he would have the other four if someone wanted to get them. I had two of my faithful customers who moved two keys a week apiece. I fronted them each five keys because I knew that they have my money straight. I then took ten keys and chopped them down into halves, quarters, and big eights because I knew that within two weeks everybody should be finished. That would leave me with six kilos that I could get my money with and that I could also use as a safety valve in case that something went wrong with someone else's business.

When Sin and Blake returned, Bo Jack and I were almost finished busting down those ten keys. It appeared to Blake that this was all that we had and that I wanted him to continue thinking that way. I took Sin into the kitchen and explained to what went on with Darren and how my plan was going down. Instead of driving to Richmond I thought that it would be best to have Darren's brother to come down with his people to pick up the work. I had Sin give him a call to let him know that it would be safer for everyone because then no one would get to know him, other than me. He agreed to do it my way and said that he would be here the following morning.

For the rest of that day the Grape Vineyard was on fire. All of my people from every surrounding city came by to get straight. Sin was sitting back and observing my flow. He was like "Now I see how Jay was getting rid of all of his work!" Sin had never been to the country before. He was amazed at how everything was so laid back. Everybody was speaking to one another and for the most part, there weren't any strangers amongst the people who came by my crib. Of course, the old heads stopped by to have drinks. Particular. He was at home away from home when he was here.

The next afternoon, Darren's brother called me when he got to Sanford. I had him and his entourage meet me at my mother's. I called up Bo Jack and had him come over so that we could transfer all of the kilos to my mother's house riding four-wheelers. By the time Darren got here we were waiting on him. To my surprise, he brought with him all of the money, including the money for the four additional keys. He said to me, "This one is for my brother, but the next one could be for us if you can make it happen again." I told him that I would check into that because from the looks of it we had created a small pipeline that was capable of making a lot of people real rich, real fast!! I promised him that I would give him a call whenever this business was complete and I had a chance to speak with Darren.

What was important to me was clearing Jay's face and helping him beat his addiction. I also informed him of my interest in his niece and he said that he could understand that because she was really a special lady.

We shook hands and I repeated to him that I would definitely get at him soon and I stressed to him how much I appreciated what he had done. He said, "I am ten grands richer and my brother is on the track to getting his life back together so really I should be thanking you."

That evening I spread the word around town that we would be hosting a barbeque in the Vineyard. We went out to the butcher store and brought pounds and pounds of food for the grills and enough beer and liquor for an army base. Before dark cars were lined up both sides of the street in front of my house and also around the block. It was all good with the neighbors because, hell, they were amongst the first people there. I had my man D.J. Fatz come from Durham to provide the music and I told him to be sure to bring his feel-good music for the old heads. I wanted Sin to see how we do it in N.C. and I could tell that he was loving every minute of it. People old and young were dancing and having a good time in the hood. The young tenders were flaunting around half dressed trying to catch the eye of the biggest ballers while the moneymakers were tossing money on the card tables trying to paint the picture that "money ain't a thang." Ol' heads like my Uncle Don and Pat were in the cut drunk as hell just having a good time. Of course, my pops was 'round about showing his ass and telling everybody that I was his son and bragging about how we set it out at our parties.

Bo Jack was back-and-forth, no drinks or chronic, I could tell that he was in a zone. I saw him talking to several different cats that were heavy in the game. I knew that he was getting off that work.

When D.J. Fatz spent his last track and crowd was diminishing, I pulled Bo Jack over so that I could speak to him privately. We went inside the garage and I asked him how things had gone because I knew that he'd been extremely busy. He said, "Hold on, I will show you because you will believe your eyes more than you will believe my mouth." He opened the back wall of the toolbox as I'd shown him the day before. All that he had left was a half of kilo. I said,

"There's no way, Bo Jack." He said to me that he issued a few deals because cats were spending so much and he told me he took the money around the block to my mother's crib. I called my mom and told her to count all of the money and place it in the "G stacks" and I would be around there as soon as everything was cleaned up and everyone was gone. Luckily for me, Sin and Blake were preoccupied by the twins, Mary and Sherry. I didn't want Blake trying to roll with Bo Jack and me. When my mom quoted the numbers to me it was enough to pay Darren and sixteen grand extra. Right then I remembered that I had forgotten to tell Bo Jack the new low prices. I was glad because now I had more money than I had expected. I told Bo Jack that whenever he got off the half a key he had left he could split the money with me 50/50 and he was like "WORD!!"

Not showing my thoughts, I couldn't believe we had sold 39 1/2 kilos within 39 1/2 hours! I didn't know if I was more happy to have taken care of Jay or more anxious to do it again so that I could pocket all of the money of Darren's that I had just looked at.

When we got back to my house Bo Jack left me and went home. Pet and Sin were in the living room smoking blunts with the twins. I was tired and had a lot to think about. I left Sin with this thought: "Call Darren in the morning and tell him to send for his car A.S.A.P. because we're ready for him and I will get at him later in the evening."

I could tell that Sin was in disbelief but he simply replied, "Ah-ite." I stretched out on my bed and tossed and turned all night long dealing with the thoughts of how to maintain my discipline. My party was fire like they normally are. I could feel the wine in the air that all the money getters knew. I had stepped my game up. I wasn't the only one. Plus, the streets talk, so it wouldn't be long before every hustler in town would know that my squad had crazy weight if they needed it. Such talk has the potential to travel from the trap to the D.A.'s office really quick and I wanted to avoid that at all costs.

I rose early the next morning and drove to my mother's

house to get the money stacks together so that I could reload Darren's toolbox and have it ready for him. Looking from the window in my garage I saw Blake and Sin pull into my yard driving Blake's car. They were joking and laughing like they were the best of friends and that was disturbing to me.

Early on I jived like Sin but when they say birds of a feather flock together, it's very true. It was no doubt that Blake was scandalous and for Sin to get so close to him so quickly it was my opinion that Sin possessed those same "double-cross" tendencies. I am a firm believer of better safe than sorry so I already knew that whenever I did business with Darren in the future I'd have to be without Sin.

Luckily I had finished loading the toolbox when the two of them arrived. I motioned for them to come inside so that I could ask Sin if he'd spoken to Darren. He told me that he had and that Darren wanted to speak with me as soon as I could call. After joking with them about the twins, I went inside of the house to call Darren.

Speaking in codes, my conversation with Darren was short and simple. I told him that I was finished and that I wanted to do the same thing again. I also asked him to make sure that Jay made good on his promise to sign himself into rehab.

Darren, on the other end of the conversation, told me that he couldn't believe that I was finished and that he would do the same thing again, with an extra grand tacked onto the end of each kilo and that he'd no doubt let Jay know that the business was complete and get him into rehab.

I thanked Darren for everything and we set up an appointment for me to meet him in Miami. I also told him that it was cool for Sin to remain in N.C. until I returned to Miami to meet with him. I told him that after our meeting it would no longer be necessary for Sin or anyone else to oversee his business with me. He told me that his people would contact me within a week or so. I had learned from this first occasion to live in expectancy because Darren wasn't a procrastinator. I understood his reasons for not giving me days or times because that was not a safe thing to do in this business!

When I hung up with Darren it was like my telephone dialed Stephanie's number. After swapping the "I miss you, boo"s, I made our conversation as short as the one that I had just made to Darren. I basically wanted her to know that she was heavy on my mind and that I planned to be back in Miami within a month. I would like to spend a couple of weeks with just the two of us. I also let her know that I'd explain everything to her in depth when we were together again. Even though she never asked questions about my business, I still knew that she had a lot of them.

She was satisfied with the short moment we spent on the phone and right as she hung up, she shocked me with a quick "Luv you!"

I returned to the garage to kick it with the fellas, but every time we got into a real conversation, someone different would pull into my driveway. I guess the previous night had been busy for everybody because one by one all of the guys that I had fronted work came by to hit me off with my money. I was trying to camouflage my business from Blake but he was extremely sharp. I stopped trying to hide what was going on. For the past two days it had been obvious to me that Blake was sensing the cold shoulder because I hadn't involved him or informed him about anything that was going on.

Since he and Sin were spending so much time building I was curious about just how much they had talked about. As much as it hurt me I just couldn't bring Blake into something this big because I'd never be able to sleep at night knowing that he could get his hands on so much money or product.

Four days later at three in the morning I was awaken by a phone call. It was a familiar voice saying to me, "Wake up, Jack, what is a gangsta doing sleep during working hours?" and he laughed. He then instructed me to look out of my window and I did just that. What I saw was another dually pulling another enclosed trailer and I was like "Awe, man, these cats are nothing but the truth." I got dressed and went outside to open my garage door so they could unhook the new trailer and to hook up to the previous one.

It was the same two drivers so they jokingly told me that I needed to slow down because if I kept up this pace I would have them on I-95 every week. I told them that I hoped it worked out that way because that would mean everybody would be eating good. After all the connections with the trailers I thought they would want to come inside to count the money and maybe even stay a night or two to get some rest. When I suggested it they both just laughed and said, "That's not the way that we operate. We like to get it over with and then rest. We will use the restroom and have a cup of coffee while we wait for you to get Sin over because Darren wants him to come back with us."

I paged Blake and when he hit me back I told him to let Sin know that he had a ride there waiting on him. When they arrived at my crib they told him to handle his business as quickly as possible because they wanted to get back on the highway.

As they were walking out of my house I saw Blake and Sin exchange numbers and I heard Blake tell him that he'd definitely be in touch with him. I thought trouble in the making but I just walked the guys to the truck and told them to have Darren hit me when he confirmed the numbers as being correct. I wouldn't be at peace until I received that confirmation.

As they drove off it left me standing alone with Blake, something that I hadn't done in so long that I didn't know what to say. It was so uncomfortable that I wanted to sit him down and put the past and present out on the table. In my heart I knew that it wasn't the time. Instead I simply told him to get at me the next evening because I needed to discuss a few things with him and Bo Jack! In actuality what I really wanted was for him to leave so that I could unload that toolbox and transfer all of its contents to my mother's house. When Blake left I didn't rest until nothing was left in my garage.

I explained to my mother that I'd be sleeping in. I went home and turned the ringer off on my phone so that I wouldn't be disturbed. I slept until close to 2:00 the next day. When I got up I didn't waste any time getting on my job. All of those stacks of money that I had just sent to Miami were my motivation because I knew that this time the stacks would belong to me. Not only did I have a vision, but I knew the vision would work if everything went as smoothly as they had on the previous job.

With that thought in mind, I didn't change a thing and I called everybody that played a part in getting off the other work. Everything from fronting work all over the streets and holding back enough to pay Darren if something went wrong, I loved the idea and it seemed to be going well. Now all I needed to do was to get my package into Richmond to Jay's brother, Corbet. I decided to let Blake take care of that. We set it up so that they could meet at a halfway point between Richmond and North Carolina. I figured it was a simple talk for Blake to make his own money and not harm anyone in the process.

For the next two weeks things went well! All of my money was rolling in, the rest of my work was on the block. Now the only person that I was waiting on was Corbet, which wasn't a problem since he had already told me that he would see me by the weekend.

I had recently leased a building and we were finishing the last of the redecorating before the grand opening of a nightclub. All of the zoning and licenses were complete and we were on schedule to opening up the next weekend. I called Corbet and told him that my club would pop from Friday until Sunday. I wanted him and his boys to spend the weekend with me to help celebrate. I also gave Dareen a call but of course the notice was too short for him because he was such a busy person. He promised to eventually stop through. Just as we were about to hang up I said to him, "By the way, I'm ready whenever you are," and he said, "I'll be in your area real soon!"

Last but not least I called Stephanie and told her that I

needed her to fly to N.C. to spend the weekend with me and I let her know it was very important. Not only did I want her to give a name to the club and to be a part of the grand opening, but I wanted to introduce her to my family! Not to mention the fact that I missed her and that I was ready to pick up where we had left off.

Being the sweetheart that she is, she agreed and told me that she'd call me later with her flight schedule. For me, it seemed things were taking shape to make for a special weekend and the beginning of a new lifestyle! In the past I'd been getting "hood money" and considered "hood rich" but I called this new income "corporate money" because it was big and flowing like water. I went from safes to safehouses and from safety deposit boxes to laundering money. It was from safety deposit boxes to laundering money, but it was all good. The new club would play a major role in cleaning up a lot of money and to provide my city with a spot for people to have a fun night out and I knew the hood would love it. No more hole-in-the-wall clubs with the entrance and exit being the same because I was about to set the city ablaze with this one.

Three dance floors, two bars, and security out of the ass to eliminate the parking lot pimping and the young guns who liked to shoot up the place. I guess you could call it grown and sexy, moneymaker that you fall back on, and that was the way that I chose to do it.

Friday morning rolled around so my mother and I drove to the airport to pick up Stephanie. They were instant best friends. I spent the ride home listening to real estate, paralegal and girl talk. I was loving the way they hit it off. When we arrived in town, we went by the club so that I could show them both around. I had decided to save myself a few trips, so I called all of my family member whom I wanted to meet Stephanie and told them to come down to the club. Everyone loved her and I understood why, because she was a very lovable person.

We went from the club to my house so that Stephanie could

unpack and get settled in for the weekend. My mother didn't give her time to rest so I told Stephanie to get it over with by allowing her to show her around and talk her ears off in the process. I told her that I had some running around to do anyways but I'd meet her back at home in two hours.

I then called Corbet and he informed me that he was on the highway and should enter my city within the hour. I gave him the exit to take, which would lead him directly to the Marriott because I was on my way out there to get three rooms for them for the weekend. I told him to ask for keys to the rooms rented in my name and I let him know the expenses were taken care of.

That is just how I do things. I set it out for my people because I expect the same from them when the tables are turned. I told him to give me a call when they were settled in and he did just that.

I shot out to the Marriott, met all of his people, and smoked so many blunts that I thought that my head would pop at any moment.

High as hell, we drove one hour to the mall and we all got fresh to death so that we would not be noticeable at the grand opening. Me being me, I had to splurge a little, so instead of stopping at the clothing and footwear stores, I decided to drop $55000.00 on an iced-out toy with a Jesus piece sitting on it. I mean, what is seven grand in the mall when I just made three quarters of a million in a little over a week?

When we arrived back in town I showed them where the club was located. I had to get home to Stephanie since I had already exceeded the two hours that I had planned to be gone. Baby understood as she always did. We weren't working with much time at that point. She was already fly but I took her by a local jewelry store to put a couple of cubes in her ear so that she'd be glistening like Daddy when we appeared on the scene.

In the car on the way to the club I asked her what did she want to name the club. She said, "Divas for the ladies and Playas for the fellas." We called it "Divas and Playas." It had a ring to it, so that it would be. When we arrived downtown to the club it was like a block party because the parking lot was to capacity as hundreds of people stood around awaiting the moment. I cut the ribbon and opened the doors. D. J. Fatz was already inside set up and getting everybody amped up with that heat that he had coming out of his speakers.

We announced the name of the club, thanked everyone for coming out, then bust the doors for the first night of action. Everyone appeared to be enjoying themselves, which made for easy money for all of the security in the building. After the last album had played, everybody exited the building in an orderly fashion and from the vibe, I could tell that we'd be doing the same thing the following night. We did except for the crowd was greater since word had spread around to surrounding areas just that quickly. I did the math from the door and the bar. The numbers had far exceeded my target numbers. There was no doubt that I could fall in love with the club thing. I made it a point to stay on my security because I didn't want any of them to slip and get relaxed because I couldn't afford to lose control of "Divas and Playas."

The weekend was winding down so Jay stopped by on his way back to Virginia. He tossed me a duffle bag full of currency and said, "How did you forget this?" I laughed and said, "Trust me, I would've thought about it as soon as I heard your voice!" When Jay hit the highway, I still had seven hours with Stephanie before I had to get her to the airport. I drove her by mother's house to say good-bye, then I took her out for dinner. Afterwards we returned to my house where I ran a hot tub of water and convinced Stephanie into allowing me to give her a sponge bath. She was shy at first but after a couple of glasses of Monet, there wasn't a shy bone left in her body. She got so loose that she started venting and telling me everything that she wanted out of life.

The more that she spoke, the bigger the teardrops got that

ran down her face. That let me know that she was speaking from her heart. Finally there was a moment of silence, I used this moment to carry her from the hot tub to my bedroom with a never thought of drying her off. I sat her down on my bed but she wouldn't unlock her arms from around me.

Instead, she rolled me over on my back and started kissing me from my lips to my chest, from my chest to my lips, but the river of tears never stopped flowing. This moment seemed out of the ordinary to me because it appeared that my dear Stephanie was begging for love more than she was begging to be made love to. This intuition that I had was so powerful that even with this beautiful, sexy, exotic woman on top of me and there for the taking, still, my nature never rose to the occasion.

I immediately stopped the progression of what probably would've happened by grabbing Stephanie's cheeks and wiping away her tears. I told her to look into my eyes and listen to me. I wanted to be all of those things to her and to be a part of all of her fantasies, but we needed to build from the ground up. I wanted to become a part of Stephanie's future but I needed her to open up her past because at some point a lot of damage had been done to her and I sensed that she needed to confide in me before we could move on with our relationship. She understood and I told her that we would make plans to spend a full week together so that we could share all of our secrets and to try to learn to confide in one another.

Stephanie got dressed and I drove her to the airport. She told me that she respected me for not being intimate with her because most men would've taken advantage of the opportunity. I assured her that there was no reason for thanks because those are the things that people do when they're trying to establish real things. As she headed for her boarding gate we hugged and kissed gently and I promised her our week would come soon.

I wrestled with myself during what seemed like a long ride home, asking myself, "What the hell were you thinking about?" I couldn't provide myself with any answers but I gave credit to my gut for stepping up because it had never led me wrong before.

Over the next six months things got extremely hectic in my life. Once I heard Jay was out of the rehab and back in Richmond and doing well, I could finally relax and really get into doing what I did. I didn't have to worry about my partner fighting his habit anymore. He had won the battle down in Miami. I pressed the throttle on my flow with Darren and I learned to let money give birth to more money by investing in any and every project that I thought would make a profit.

I was eating on every set and before long a lot of the love that I was receiving in different turned into mean mugs. What really woke me up to the hating and larceny was a two-part event that happened within two hours of each other.

First, I was at my aunt's house playing some friendly ten-twenty tunk with a couple of the cats from my hood. The homie "Blink" was there and unfortunately for him "Lady Luck" wasn't on his side. He lost all of his money. Blink was a big guy, around 6'3" and 220 pounds. He was very dangerous! He had been in and out of prison since he was a juvenile. All of his crimes were considered violent. He had lost a lot of weight and started robbing people on the block. The word on the streets was that he was getting high off of crack!

I never changed the way that I carried it with the people that I grew up around. It wasn't unusual to find me at such events. Once Blink lost his money he sat around until he saw that I was about to leave. He asked me to give him a ride home. I agreed, but once in the car he started to say weird things like "Since you have over a grip on your neck, it'd seem like you'd give your struggling homie his money back!" I told him that I don't know what he was getting at and I had nothing but love for him, but I let him know that I was strapped and that he needed to dead that thought.

He then downsized it as if he shouldn't have ever entertained that thought. I knew that he had it in his heart to rob me. Later that night as I sat in my living room, I observed two guys run down beside my house. Sensing that I saw them, Blink and his stickman came to the screen door and knocked. With my nine in my hand I walked to the door and spoke to them through the door. I told them that they needed to find someplace else to do them because what they had on their minds could definitely get someone hurt.

I had already calculated jealousy but I had to factor in greed. If my own homeboy coveted my stacks, then I knew that I couldn't put it past the next man. I decided to move to the country and not show anyone where I lived.

I had all of my lieutenants in order so basically my business ran itself. I was seldom seen in the hood because most of my time was spent with different females around the way. Seven days meant seven freaks and seven magnums. That didn't leave much time to think about Stephanie.

During those days I used to sex these women just because and then ruin happy homes without any conscience. I guess that I was too young to understand the seriousness of these acts and the pain that I was causing in these relationships.

This one cat in particular probably still hates me today for sleeping with his mother and his baby mother within days, but it was just one of those things. I had a history with his child's mother so that wasn't unusual but my encounter with his mother was like a "freak event" you would see on Nip Luck! I was at a cousin's house and his mother Tina was on the phone talking to someone in the house. She shocked me even further when she asked to come over to my house. I gave her directions to my house, not thinking that she would really come over. I went home just in case.

An hour later, to my surprise, Tina pulled into my driveway in her van. It was a light drizzle outside. I stood in my door and watched her speed walk in her heels to my porch. Once inside the first thing that she asked was if we were here alone. I told her yes and for her to sit down. I was about to ask her if I could get her a drink or anything and before I could ask she had removed the long trench coat that she was wearing. She hung it on the coatrack.

The removal of the coat wasn't what tied my tongue but the fact that she only had on a full-length lace body suit underneath the coat. The midsection of the body suit was cut out and it had me standing as stiff as a zombie. Little did she know that I could remember having fantasies about her as a teenager. The body that she had back then hadn't lost one of its curves. As I was standing there staring, thinking to myself that she was older than my mother, I thought, what am I gonna do? She solved that by saying, "My husband will be home in two hours and I will need to be there!"

Once inside my bedroom she asked if I was into receiving oral sex! Already intimidated by her maturity I caught myself stuttering as I told her that I would never receive it!!! With an aggressive but sensual voice she told me, "This is gonna be something that you'll never forget," and she instructed me to get a tray of ice cubes from my refrigerator! Needless to say it was a moment that I still remember.

She had me so open that she could call me at any hour and I would get out of my bed to meet her any place that she wanted. It got the point that I had to wean myself from her because as much as I loved being with her I couldn't continue sleeping with another man's wife and a classmate's mother.

The last time that I was with Tina we were having a pillow talk discussing how it would be the last time that we would be together in that way. I received a 911 page from an 804 area code. I knew right away that it was from Richmond. I quickly placed the call and it was Corbett, Jay's brother, telling me that Blake had been arrested just outside of Richmond.

I went by my mother's house to pick up ten stacks in case I had to pay a bondsman. I hopped in my Cadillac and headed to Donnel's, alone. My nerves running rapid, I sparked a blunt just to get a peace of mind. Although Blake was scandalous I still didn't want him spending one night in jail, at least if there was something that I could do to prevent it.

When I arrived in Richmond, I sat down with Donnell and he briefly described to me the details involving Blake's situation. After making numerous trips to Virginia Blake had acquired a few friends in the Church Hill section of Richmond. I remind you, Blake likes to stunt so it didn't surprise me when I heard that he'd won some money from some guys gambling and rubbed it in a little too much.

The word that reached Donnell was the guys got a little fatigued from his victory celebration and decided to take back their losings. Blake was able to reach his hammer and prevent being robbed. However, once he left the premises one of those busters called the police, gave a description of Blake's car, and informed the officers that a felon was in possession of a firearm.

There you have it, Blake was pulled, searched, and charged for being a felon in possession of a firearm. Donnell's niece called the magistrate's office to find out what Blake's bond was. They told her it was only $7500.00. We sent her down there to bail him out. While Meka, Donnell's niece, went to pick up Blake, Donnell and I discussed any attorneys that he knew. He had a relative who practiced law in the city so we gave him a call. We explained to him that we needed his services. He agreed to take the case and instructed us to bring Blake by his office the following day. It hadn't been my plan to spend a night in Richmond, but since it was necessary I didn't have a problem with it. Of course, Donnell opened his home for us but I opted to get me and Blake a room at a nearby hotel. I wanted to get a feel for his mindset. It had been years since Blake and I had been isolated together in one spot. I figured that it was due time.

We left Donnell's and stopped by a local department store to buy an alarm clock to wake us up early enough to go buy some gear for our appointment the next morning. We went to our room and rolled two blunts as we discussed his charges and reminisced about our past. It had been a long time since we laughed together and I missed it but I still couldn't see him as the Blake of old who stood beside me with the "Troop Four" jacket. Even as I laughed with him on that night and listened to him give an account of his evening I felt a vibe that something wasn't right. His story wasn't adding up for me. I blamed it on the hydro that we were smoking and the fact that I just didn't trust Blake.

The next morning after we bought clothes we showered and went to a popular restaurant for breakfast. Donnell met us there so we could follow him to his relative's office. Once Donnell introduced us to him Blake turned to us and said that he would rather speak to the lawyer alone. We were like "Okay" because we didn't see it as a big deal.

After about 45 minutes they returned from the office and I quickly got a rad of Malcolm, the lawyer. He had a look on his face that lacked confidence but Blake's expression didn't match. Blake pulled me to the side and told me that Malcolm wanted five grand to represent him. Malcolm played golf with the D.A.; he was confident that he could get his case thrown out. Without hesitation I went to the caddy to grab five stacks so that we could find our way back to N.C.

When I handed Malcolm the money I could still see the look in his eyes. I didn't dwell on it because I knew that once I left Virginia I had done all that I was supposed to do for Blake.

For the next few weeks Blake was hanging around my house a lot. It was like he thought that things were back to our childhood days. Since he had a case pending I wasn't putting any work in his possession. I didn't want to be a part of him catching another charge.

I had my man Steve making those runs but I made sure that Blake's pocket was healthy at all times. He was dating a girl named Juanita. I had dated her in high school. I could tell that they were getting serious.

From time to time I would need him to do some cooking so I would call him. Blake could always be reached at Juanita's crib. Once

I told him that I was coming by her house to speak to him but he told me that he would meet me up the street. It was funny to me because I knew that he was keeping me out of Juanita's presence.

Pride wouldn't allow him to share with Juanita how issues were growing in his life and it was easy for him to conceal because I never let him fall off.

Juanita and I were still friends and we spoke secretly sometimes. We always stayed on the level. She would tell me how Blake proclaimed to be the boss and that Bo Jack and I worked for him. She would laugh and say, "Why does the boss still live at home?" It was all good, though, because it wasn't my thing to touch a lady who was involved with any of my homies. By Blake being heartless, he didn't understand my code. He once accused me of sleeping with Juanita. She had a party in Raleigh with only a few of her friends in attendance.

Blake was supposed to meet me and Steve there. We were going to buy some things for the party but he never showed up. After paging him numerous times, I gave. I drove Juanita and her friends to the liquor store. I wasn't stunting but I let Juanita know that she could order whatever she wanted because she was a real friend to me. She wasn't a stranger to money but I could see her friend's eyes light up with dollar signs each time a rubber band would pop. Steve and I stayed in Raleigh that night with two of Juanita's friends. Blake assumed that I had stayed the night with Juanita. As childish as it sounded, I called the girl that I had spent the night with so that she could tell Blake that I was with her and not Juanita.

I allowed that situation die because I knew that Blake was under a lot of duress dealing with his situation in Richmond. It didn't make things any easier for him because he tried to hide things from his mother also.

Like I had predicted years earlier, the shady side of Blake began to resurface. He came by my house one Friday morning but I wasn't home. He left a message with a girl name Meka who had been staying with me for a few months that he'd be back around 4:30 P.M. Meka and I were doing our thing but she was only living with me temporarily because she had some problems at home.

Meka and Blake had experienced the "childhood crush" together but I had discussed this with him before I indulged. He gave me the okay because they never had any relations.

Anyway, like promised, he returned at 4:30 P.M. to speak with me. He had seen an Acura Legend for $3500.00 that he wanted me to buy for him. Without hesitation I walked him to my bedroom and pulled four grand from the stash and gave it to him. He had his cousin with him named Cake. He was an associate of Steve's.

Later that night Cake whispered to Steve that Blake was going to get as much from me as he could because he felt that I was only being generous to him to prevent him from mentioning my name.

Until he made that statement that hadn't been a thought of mine but now it was something to think about. He couldn't make such a statement if it wasn't a thought of his. I instantly pressed the panic button. I called Darren and shut down all operations.

I decided to go to my uncle's for a few drinks and since Meka was staying with a friend, I told her to take the other eleven grand from the house with her because Blake had seen where I kept it. When I returned from my uncle's I was twisted from shots of B & E! I went into my kitchen and noticed the window of my back door had been busted out. I went to my coupe and grabbed my 45. I searched the house to make sure that no one was inside.

After making sure that I was alone in the house, I returned to the back door. Strangely enough, the glass was on the back porch, which meant that the window was broken from inside of the house.

From there I went to the bathroom to find that the window was not locked. I knew that it was an inside job. I remembered that Blake had used the bathroom before he let. He became my number-one suspect. Thinking of my money, I went to the spot that I had placed it. The money was gone.

I called Meka to ask her if she had taken the money with her and she told me that she had forgotten to take it. When she asked if everything was alright, I assured her that it was because I didn't want to be the first to speak on what had happened.

I figured that if I didn't mention it to anyone, the only people who could talk about it were the people that were involved. I went and got an older friend of mine. We called Alley Cat to tape my window until the next day. We would have to replace the whole window. I looked at my caller I.D. and I saw that Blake had called around ten P.M. It puzzled me because Meka and I were both home at 10:00 P.M. Curiosity caused me to page him and when he called back he told me that he hadn't called me. I didn't tell him that I saw his number on the box.

Maybe I was tripping but I could've sworn that I had heard the same music playing in the background from when I called Meka's cell phone. I let the thought pass because I really needed some rest.

The next morning I had Alley Cat drive me to a country hardware store to buy another door. As we drove down the highway, Blake was driving toward us. Someone on the passenger side ducked their head as if hiding. I had Alley Cat turn around. Blake was speeding trying to get away. I granted him his wish and turned on the street that Meka's friend lived on. Meka's car was in the yard so I knocked on the door. Her friend Shon answered the door. She looked shocked to see that it was me knocking on the door. I said, "Where's Meka?" She told me that she had gone to the store with her sister and that she would have her page me as soon as she returned. I calmly said alright because I didn't want anyone to think that I was suspicious.

Alley Cat and I returned home and put the door in place. As soon as he finished Meka drove up. When she came inside I could tell that she didn't know what to expect. I didn't give her any indication that I was suspicious. I had come to the conclusion that she and Blake were creeping.

While she was doing some things in the bedroom, I cleared the caller I.D. box. I looked at my watch as if I had an appointment and asked her if Blake had called while she was on the phone the night before. When she said that he hadn't, I knew the deal. I pretended to be naïve because if I alarmed either one of the two, it could hurt me.

Alley Cat needed to get home so I told him to drive as I took the shotgun position to twist me a philly. All types of thoughts plagued my brain, even thoughts of Stephanie. Still, I couldn't understand what it was that was holding me back from pursuing what appeared to be the perfect woman for me.

Instead of going straight home Alley Cat wanted to stop by to see his daughter Renee. It was cool with me because I was always in the mood to see a pretty face. Renee and I had a mirage of a relationship. Most people did not know how to take us. Her brother was my cousin and her dad had spent so much time with me that everyone thought that we were related. Even her boyfriend whom she lived with thought that we were cousins. Behind closed doors we would often flirt but we kept it honest because we were actually very close friends. On that particular day when she came out to the car, she could tell that I had a lot on my mind. She asked if I needed to talk and I nodded yes. She told her mother to pick her up in an hour.

We left and I took Alley Cat home to handle his business. We then went to my house so that I could handle my business. Alley Cat took the Cadillac to pick up Renee with instructions to meet me at my mother's house. I got fresh to death and hopped in the coupe to pick Renee up. She was "fly" as usual. We left for Durham with nothing out of the ordinary on our minds.

During our drive there she told me that her boyfriend expected her to be with her dad all night. That was like music to my ears because I needed a little out of town air. Durham was my home away from home. I took Renee by the mall to get some things since she didn't pack an overnight bag. I had a spot in Durham so I was good, but it was close to impossible for me to walk through a mall without dropping off a stack. What was meant to be a quick stop for a few items turned out to be an hour-long laughing spree mixed with a lot of shopping.

I didn't mind buying Renee things because she was not a gold digger. In the short time that we'd left home I was already feeling better. It was still early and our fun was far from being over. A friend of mine lived minutes from the mall so we stopped by his house to let him know that I would be in town until the next day.

That visit didn't last long because when he opened his door the dog ran out. I did not know that Renee had a canine phobia. Neither did I know about her 20-inch vertical until she leaped onto the hood of my coupe yelling at the top of her voice. It wasn't funny at the time but it was our joke for the rest of the evening.

We remained on the level of our normal outings until Renee came out of the shower wearing that "pink thing" that I had bought her earlier from the mall. All day long she'd spoken encouraging words in my ear like an angel. Now she appeared to be one outwardly. In the past we'd spent numerous nights together and at times shared the same bed without becoming intimate. It wasn't going down like that on this night.

At first we laid beside each other in bed and talked like two siblings who hadn't seen each other in a while. We were catching up on secrets that we hadn't shared and discussed but then it happened. The eye contact that became the silent language that was interpreted by me as "I wish that you'd come and take me right now!!" My response was that her wish would be granted...needless to say that all boundaries of our relationship were removed that night. We made love until we were both drenched with sweat. We both agreed that it was long overdue and decided that it would be good for the both of us to implement sex into our relationship, permanently.

It had been a while since I had seen Renee. I was sure that

her thoughts matched mine. We both knew what to expect when I saw her.

Two months had passed with no work and no word from Blake about his case. Unfortunately for the partygoers, my club had conveniently been shut down due to its increase in violence. I wasn't exactly a happy camper but I was a curious one.

Following my intuitions, I decided to search Blake's soul by getting into his head a little. Out of the blue I called him up and asked him to take a ride with me. I pulled out the toy, my dark blue three-and-a-quarter, and let the convertible top back. When I stopped by to scoop Blake I already had two blunts filled to the max sitting in the ashtray and 2Pac's "Thug Life" C.D. banging out the song system.

As we smoked the blunts I drove Blake through the Vineyard and all the spots that we used to hang out. We arranged them from our youth to our adulthood. Judging from his silence and gestures I could tell that he was reminiscing on how things used to be. To end this joyride I pulled into the garage and got out of the car. I sat on the hood with my blunt in my hand. Blake got out and joined me. I said to him, "This was my life, this is my life, and it will continue to be my life until someone takes it from me."

We got back in the car and I drove him home and told him that I'd get at him later. As he exited my car he turned and asked, "What was that all about?" With a low but sincere voice I told him that I remembered where we came from but unfortunately many others didn't. I left him on that note and with that thought.

I went by the barbershop to get a fade and to chop it up with the fellas. When I was in the chair my Aunt Kim's number vibrated my pager with a 911 suffix!! Without hesitation I called her to find out the rollers had kicked in her door with a search warrant. She told me they left with the same things that they came with. I finished my cut, then went to her house. Before I could put my feet on the ground my auntie came running to the passenger side telling me to go to my mother's house.

When we got there all I saw were black jackets and alphabets climbing around inside of my mother's garage. Inside the ceiling I had prepared a bait for Blake. I let Aunt Kim out when we were out of the police's sight. I wanted to gather details. I went to my house to get some money away in case my house was next on the hitlist. When I finished lining the door panels of my low-low I called my mothers to get a report. Aunt Kim answered and told me they took a stolen Kawasaki that I had in the garage and a big-screen television from inside of the house. Thinking of bigger things I had forgotten about the smaller things. There was no use dwelling on it because they had the stolen goods.

I hopped into the low-low and headed to my stash house down in the country. I thought no one knew about it. Looking into my rearview mirror I felt that I was being followed. The car that I had pinpointed faded away. I charged it to paranoia. I continued my route to my stash house. Getting out of the car I realized that I didn't think to grab my key to the house. I would have to enter through a bedroom window. Doing so I quickly got inside and came to the front door. I could exit and bring the money from the car.

When I opened the door and stepped out onto the porch I wasn't alone anymore. Ten cars, thirty police, and a tow truck with my motorcycle on the back were all there with me.

The weed that I had smoked earlier still had me calm. I walked out to the awaiting calvary with my hands up. Routinely they threw me down and cuffed me as half of them ripped my car apart and the other half began remodeling my stash house. I knew they'd find the money in the car but I was confident that they had no chance on finding the two keys I kept hidden in the walls as a safety valve. As predicted, they exited my property emptyhanded and only charged me with possession of stolen goods. They even let me follow them to the police station to stand before the magistrate and sign my own bond.

After being riddled by all the police threats I jumped inside my car to head home. To my disbelief the police didn't even see the money that was right in their face inside my car. How blind are they and how lucky am I, I thought! With all the mounting pressures it was beginning to feel like the walls were closing in on me.

Time to face my demons. I rested all but 10 minutes after getting home before Blake's lawyer called from VA. A little rattled by the call I decided to pick up to hear what news was on the other end. By the way my day was going I was expecting the worse. To my surprise he went on to tell me he had managed to strike a deal with the DA where Blake wouldn't receive a felony and he would only have to do 60 days in the county jail for the gun, problem being he'd spoken to Blake prior to calling me and he was hesitant about accepting the deal. Blake had never been away from home before so the news wasn't sitting well on his stomach. His lawyer wanted me to speak to Blake to see if I could convince him to take the plea deal because a jury trial could land him in prison for 36 months. I assured him I'd speak to Blake!

Growing up with Blake and knowing him the way I did I knew I'd have to use a special tactic in order to convince him that 60 days wasn't such a bad deal.

Never a heavy weed smoker I decided to take a whole blunt to the head in order to get my mind right. I gave Blake a call and asked him to meet me at Ruby Tuesdays for a few drinks, he agreed.

After a few shots and a few laughs I got straight to the point. Taking the lead and saying everything on my mind was the way you had to do with Blake. Unexpectedly I took him back to the Troop JACKETS. I explained to him how I had known all these years how he had betrayed me back in the day. Before he could speak, I went on to apologize to him for holding that inside for so many years. I admitted to him the wall I had built between us and kept him away from any deals I felt were major. I told him we were older now and facing situations we didn't need to deal with alone. I told him I loved him and extended my hand to him to symbolize a new beginning. He took the high road by apologizing to me also and told me it hadn't happened since and would never happen again. A toast to new beginnings! New beginnings meant a new way of life and a fresh start. I explained to Blake. I made a pact with him that if he'd go put Richmond behind us I'd put together a plan for all of us. He already knew I had his back in all of his affairs for the couple months he'd be away. He quickly agreed it was the best thing for him. So we had a couple more drinks and appetizers and called it a night.

Today, 8-27-20

Ironically today was day 1 of Blake's sentence and also day 1 of Jay's sobriety. These were my guys and I would do anything necessary to get them both on the right track. What I knew was, making positive plans for them would lead me into positive waters. I spoke to Stephanie this morning and told her my plan was to move to Miami with her once Blake was released from jail. She was all for that and said she was going to hold me to that promise. By the time these next 59 days passed Jay would either have won or lost his battle. I was confident he would be the winner he'd been since I met him. I would be in constant contact with him and I was sure it would be an inspiration to him just knowing I would be down in Florida soon.

I have never been without the drug game but there's a time and a season for everything. It took me until now to realize that you're only a leader when you can get a leader to follow you. In a time when the police would rather murder a black on TV as opposed to arresting him, I think it's best to put the game to rest. Who knows where this next chapter of life will carry us but I'm determined to lead us to prosperity!